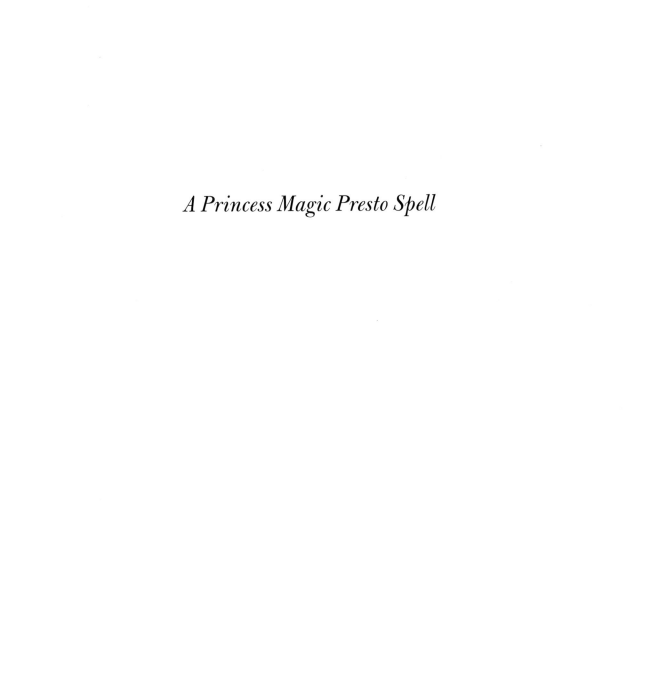

A Princess Magic Presto Spell

ALSO BY LISA JARNOT

A Princess Magic Presto Spell

Lisa Jarnot

with artwork by Emilie Clark

SOLID OBJECTS

NEW YORK

Grateful acknowledgment is made to The Song Cave and City Lights Publishers for publishing portions of this work previously.

Art by Emilie Clark:
p. 7: untitled EHR-35, from *Sweet Corruptions*, 2012
p. 13: untitled BBG-4, from *My Garden Pets*, 2010
p. 19: untitled BBG-6, from *My Garden Pets*, 2010
p. 23: untitled BBG-11, from *My Garden Pets*, 2010
p. 27: untitled BBG-14, from *My Garden Pets*, 2010
p. 31: untitled Mt-M3, from *Home Studies in Nature*, 2005

Design by Erik Rieselbach

Printed in Canada

ISBN-10: 0-9844142-7-4
ISBN-13: 978-0-9844142-7-7

SOLID OBJECTS
P. O. Box 296
New York, NY 10113

Part One

Amedellin Cooperative Nosegay

Into the eve of a picnic of trees of the strawberry rugulet rabbit tyrone
into a glazed economic disturbance caused by the rain most dramatic and strange
    small whole moon in the sky   fishlike in semblance
    as damp as an amphibrach the anthony braxton gland of ant launch

      wind-blown shutters   angry household gods   wet september horses
    schubert's trout quintet   (shy franz schubert)   two german shepherds
      al qaeda in flushing   and *earth's microphone willy-nilly*

into the eve of   *multitudinous seas incarnadine*   all one word: shy franz schubert yuki lily atkins
      feverish hippo zion   fallen giraffe incident

and the mysteries:

christ, death, genitals, the stimulation phase, salivation of the lamb, william partridge orange, boring dutch milkmaid, the paranormal finger, seven west 46th street's aristocratic vagueness panda, turquoise buddha henpeck pacification, fleckner sarkis bop, object relations banana, offending purple snowsuit, pegma and plengg

with tender purloined sunlight
at winter's lip

specializing in yellow
starlings in flight
over arthur's seat

this very linty cow
that useless tibetan babysitter
the prime meridian a pale dead moose in the sky
into the eve of a picnic of trees
of the strawberry rugelet rabbit tyrone

tenemos par chinches
helen mirren naked running from what

the wild screaming beaches of the ancient mariner, his dutch husband and four mosques by the by an ermine trouser snake over the rainbow of red meat hedonisms, get rich quick, lose weight now pasha parker penguin

and on brick lane
a television fell
from a lorry
we bought it
for fifty quid

waves of sleep a lovely lincoln, albuterol, first snow

this state sponsored car alarm, my lost mason jar, vivian rose champion's delicate victorian ankles, the lonely bird, autumnal burnings, duncan's, cold and clear,

while slyly coffee hangs
outside below a
wall of snow

on bodega dust: include emancipatory relationships, odyssia's very original boobs and the warm apt facts of john thaw, ham, and train stations, this moon dewed glass, this small moon, this ba ba ba (first instance of) grandmother in grave these fleeting forms: very gentle sikh, book of penis, italians in florida, and allen also

register individual mayweed, harvey, jack, and bob, robert, jess, and stan, anne's red noir, lonely frank o'hara, perpetual free actuaries, almost actual giraffe, humorless minimalist electronica, very linty cow, medicated american individualists this plantain a modest garden, kate mcgarrigle also, three guinea hens, very linty sunrise, four latin grannies and domenica with a new calendar, lonely nina simone, a very gray day, the case of the missing stamps, a foot massagenist, and the creation of earls

leap over a
large rock splendored
with april moss

for the sea, sailing, and the french revolution, pines and pineapples, gumming finger food and winter cress with weapons grade literature his fiancée jane sewing chickens together the sparrows in the cherry tree, the hedgehogs in the chanterelle bin, locust and bartleby: first two worlds, blender, air conditioner, guinea pig and the pedestrian on queens boulevard, a wriggler, I, all of nature, an occasional seagull, howth castle environs, a pale dead moose in the sky, an idiot in cat suit, an afghan ameer, the persian empire and two mathildas

cher dumps me (in a dream) a disregarded entity in wiggim's forest, a tittie rizzle, after the z, after the e, a luminous simultaneity, silver and hearts prophet mohammed in a bear suit, an omelet corner, my actual entity, my baby bear, my presentational immediacy, my beach plum, in blue lobelia, for mary osborne, this year and the next that is scented vaguely of potatoes

there was too
much of lester
in that room

9

removed his caterer in the koreas

a ready-made world, salerno's water buffalos,
the lemon sun in the sky
the silver cat in the nepeta

and lewis's mother
william blake's mother
sun ra's space world
the sixth extinction
this, peter's banjo
that, allen's harmonium
what do you
know about chickens
about sadness and
raspberry jam and
the hundred thousand
songs of milarepa
a molecular empathy
plinkets of sunlight
connecting all the
stars

bebe con queso with very many steps, very many g's, a weary charlotte prodger washing birds while high on marijuana, beautiful gingko trees here and there, toughest well ever, a something oxbow,

old fashioned hominid

yes, to have
a favorite place

into the eve of a picnic of trees
of the strawberry rugulet rabbit tyrone

contemplative roommate wanted: no snow globes, that new things happen in the equinox with a baby named ellington, brad will's laundry (in a dream) call me hester drooping joe-pye weed,

for her now
a wood mite
white sweet clover

pale dead tree in the sky,
the whirled imperfect

while bumble bees
breakfast in the
lamb's ear's stalks

own some land
have some trees
google in indonesia

(in a dream)

land of wheels   dominated by sycamores

we talked about fish for hours
faggots, pie, bacon,

then sudden rain,   *forgotten monkey amber*

the catalpa tree, filthy third-world playground, alder, hazel, pine, an italic gait, an antediluvian world,

deep metaphysical fatigue
beautiful but stupid
and tuli also

that we slip
into and out
of the world

companions, mud, adversity,

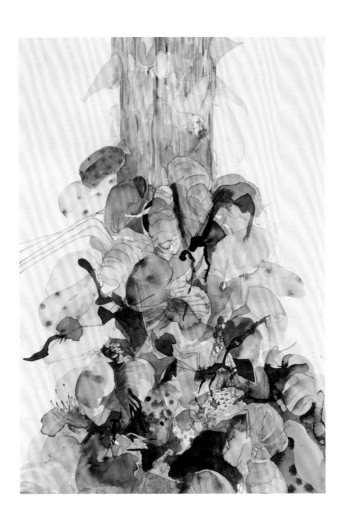

two snow monkeys,
two rabid beavers,
poor franz kafka

these ancient macaroons
and huge victorian fairies

my baby bear
my gorgeous goose
my beach plum

an occasional lycanthropy mcdonalds
in leroy
with ghost-free rooms
white sweet clover
water of. night!

Part Two

A Boa Constructor

Thomas, bring soap,
           a fear of chipmunks   the end of restaurants   bears in dumpsters,
                                   cucumber, apple, and mint

                           on friendly street
                           the honey bees,
                           the ash trees'
                               flash of amber

around the corners of the day,
a ghost arbor:
october's aster shadows

                    say quercus borealis,
                    the leaf torn
                    from its tit

first k sound,
      milk, apple, cracker,

  trapped chilean miners in a
    spectacularly disappointing universe,
                    peabok sea quay   peking duck house

  a plodder, I
        a globular body
        derived from the
        voice of a

                bird, rock, ring

perplexed by sheep, *dance, art, owls,*

        the penguin listening
        to the gramophone

dance, art cow!   *eat and dance!*

of the emperor
and his genitals

of a hungry
oaxacan space dog

of an under-aged
 moroccan pole-dancer

     owl   *ice*   *owl*

a yam diva,
        sea lions, mongooses, alpacas,

            I keep a chart with stars, "heap" for "sleep",
        portuguese cuddle-up time and nancy samstein's sheep
        (in a dream)

those legends of the jews, these tales of hoffman, a newton pippin and sally heming's offspring,
spectral electrical reindeer imperatives: *walk, dance, eat, sleep, peep, turtle, rabbit, deer,*

        the color of the desert
        reflected in the fatigues
        of an ortiz

the midnight milkless melancholy of an icy beaver oracle

the case of the elusive tricycle
the return of the quiche-eating moose
a stammering king
enunciates a k
to a new throbbing congress

this mole, that badger, this rat, low blue lobelia in a dream where someone died
and left elton john in charge,
        an octurnal nowl
          in a kite of neige

         neck   *fork*   *tail*

this debauched kinesthesia
that big dream porn book

        welcome to the land of rodney,
        honey, ennui, pie

       nice   *shirt*   *moon*

    a whispered "ah" of a funny red seagull

that it must have
    recesses, a room designed such

the translucent gray elkhart dawn-light of
lori's colon, danny's job, karen's pedicure,
karen's mother's cell phone conversation

no horse
no owl

one minky jeoffrey link
fourteen camelback locomotive ox carts
a red maple velcro mama
and gloria wong's life coach

I see you, camels, I see you copernicus triangle food odyssey,

that seventy-nine commandos
and a dog were involved

that they blew some people up and down

catch it!
stop it!
go there!
I want to do that,

in june's white wet
lilt of leaf

have courage, mr. wang
have a big house, a yellow telephone, a blue car,
have *mango turkey boobie*

the first *why*, the first *what*, the *what that he's doing*, the *what is that*, the *who else*, and
what happened are you okay?

a wood mite
a cabbage white
I'll fly it away
and men say yay

and where is he? and where is she?

michael, rynn, kari,
akilah, brad, and someday harry.

hydrangeas and helicopters
                    grief its proper mode

"d" in "death"
under the space between
"will" and "remember"

that it smells like the painting of a flower

a red flower
a pink kid
a blue dude
and pythons
eating strawberries.

Part Three

Every Body's Bacon

Eating the carrots   *I'm happy like this*   *I don't wear underwear*   *I love pizza*
I think about guppies all the time

pale fawn fluff of these first winter beans
of george the fifth's one thousand pheasants
of those morning glories   those peach trees
those rain storms and those floods

of the sangha   the dharma the buddha
and of edward over there,

not a gibbon, not a gorilla, just a new moon waxing   squiggly and recalcitrant
where *the sun is getting up,   so up yours—*
it's not a tigger,   *it's a sea otter*   *a mosquito that goes tra la la*   a ravioli satire gate,
a leaping squirrel on cedar hill   the taxi, sparrow, kitten

poor night owl

white snake root—

a cat's empty bowl places the stars in the sky.

I'm a quiet drunk, a timid bicyclist, a decent gardener,
I'm a mama dressed up like a papa,
an orning mug, a hungry bud,
a hypoepic nodule of occult origin

I display nine reservations about the sprawling metropolis

can you believe that the sun has eyes
that ted is gone,
that harry's not here,
that pierre was pulled from the paper pile

can you believe that this is a beautiful house
it has toys and butterflies, and cups—

you call nestor, I'm going to dance,

poor half moon in the sky
fearless and joyful
with *monks not monkeys*

into the eve of a picnic of trees
of the strawberry rugelet rabbit tyrone

sahashra enzo rust in an otter box of solstice coot, *look at that beautiful child glowing in the night*, for small art, for saxon churches, defiant lightness, take a restless optimism, a wanky thing, and peale's mastodon, find the train to cockfosters, the hearth smoke, the bread, the nettles, the starlings eating puke, take the sock poet, for example, that other smashed pine cone, those three kings' camels, the word "malvas" in a dream; remember dave's wang, an abner's ashes, and paul revere

In the war I have made a celestial cave, a big womble, a liverpool wappingen picture, an annual guide to jewish genetic disease,

in the war I have made a fem pop ass crack cancer of the whole rabbit coming, of the grackles in the ramble at the rabbi's house,

say pancakes, carrots, and nutcases,
              pink chimp pansies,
          a massalinging hoco,

greet the first autonomous art of the equinox   easter broccoli aphids rise   to a mouse that tastes like art
          starting to enjoy doing nothing   sitwell, edith,   the desiccated pussy of,
              come sleep on this big hippo,   *all over him*

              write silly gilly gumball,
              be not in the mood of crab,
              not in the mood of octopus,
              not in the mood of avocado,
              of starlings in flight (in a dream)

     with the chickens
     they have made
     a celestial cave,

          with dr. bragg's anubis,
          with corn, oars, honey,
          and the door,

write silly gilly gumball,
a chamomile bluejay
and lactose intolerant neanderthals

to wash it with toast, the chillingly dark song of a hero ed park tree hest stick conkle salami pirate vessel— *I see their little lanterns,* I say their little slither, *I like tripping so rainbows come out of my mouth I'm pregnant with guinea pigs and hamsters and trees,*

and when the honey rises,
they make honey shoes,
a wilkinson wallachia that causes all the meows,

I will line up in the sentence, merrily, cross-fire, *when I was big like I am,* I see "montage" for "mortgage", a cigarette, roses, and poop, "Jamaica" for "Judaism", *a bank robert* in spitzer's walnut room,

I see the coronal ejection mass of the helleborism of the ancients, of my bird fred, of henry needham, carpenter, of petrinkus the frog, the premier posek of a generation,

I will line up in the sentence of this lonely vehiculate, a day leaning toward evening, a midsummer cacophony of peaches, hydrangeas, and bees,

a vanya, oh,
an anca tudor,
a princess magic presto spell.

August 23, 2009 – July 27, 2012

LISA JARNOT is the author of five full-length books of poetry, including *Joie de Vivre: Selected Poems 1992–2012* (City Lights, 2013). Her *Robert Duncan: The Ambassador from Venus* was nominated for a National Book Critics Circle Award in 2012. She lives in Jackson Heights, Queens, with her husband and daughter.

EMILIE CLARK has exhibited her work at the Nevada Museum of Art in Reno, the Lynden Sculpture Garden in Milwaukee, the Children's Museum of the Arts in New York, the San Jose Museum of Art, the Weatherspoon Museum, and elsewhere. Her work has been featured in many publications, including *Bomb*, *Printed Project*, and *Cabinet Magazine*.